TEAM STUDIES ON CHARACTER VOLUME 5

Rod Handley and Gordon Thiessen

ISBN 1-929478-95-X

Cross Training Publishing
www.crosstrainingpublishing.com
(308) 293-3891

All scripture quotations are taken from the Holman Christian Standard Bible, Copyright 1999, 2000,2002, 2003 by Holman Bible Publishers. Used by permission. Holman Christian Bible, Holman CSB and HCSB are federally registered trademarks of Holman Bible Publishers. This book is manufactured in the United States of America.

Library of Congress Cataloging in Publication Data in Progress.

I am a Christian first and last.
I am created in the likeness of God Almighty to bring Him glory.
I am a member of Team Jesus Christ. I wear the colors of the cross.

I am a Competitor now and forever. I am made to strain, to stretch and
to succeed in the arena of competition. I am a Christian Competitor
and as such, I face my challenger with the face of Christ.

I do not trust in myself, I do not boast in my abilities or believe in
my own strength. I rely solely on the power of God. I compete for
the pleasure of my Heavenly Father, the honor of Christ and
the reputation of the Holy Spirit.

My attitude on and off the field is above reproach – my conduct beyond criticism.
Whether I am preparing, practicing or playing: I submit to God's authority
and those He has put over me. I respect my coaches, officials, teammates,
and competitors out of respect for the Lord.

My body is the temple of Jesus Christ. I protect it from within and without.
Nothing enters my body that does not honor the Living God.
My sweat is an offering to my Master. My soreness is a sacrifice to my Savior.

I give my all – all of the time. I do not give up.
I do not give in. I do not give out. I am the Lord's warrior – a competitor by conviction
and a disciple of determination.
I am confident beyond reason because my confidence lives in Christ.
The results of my efforts must result in His glory.

Let the competition begin. Let the glory be God's.

Sign the Creed @ www. fca.org

CONTENTS

CONTACTING THE AUTHORS

Rod Handley
Character That Counts
512 NE Victoria Drive
Lee's Summit, MO 64086
www.characterthatcounts.org

Gordon Thiessen
Cross Training Publishing
P.O. Box 1874
Kearney, NE 68848
www.crosstrainingpublishing.com

To contact FCA or order FCAGear
call 1-800-289-0909 or
check us out on the web at FCA.org

Team Studies on Character Volume 1, 2, 3, 4
are also available as well as an expanded edition,
Character that Counts for Athletes Volume 1, 2, 3

PREFACE

How do I use this book? This book is designed to help you and your teammates build your character. In FCA we call this type of discussion a Team Huddle. It is important that you take enough time during your meetings (approximately 29-40 minutes) to go through each section of the Huddle meeting. Each week you will have the opportunity to talk about how you were able to build your character since the previous Team Huddle. After this time of catching up, you will do a warm up to introduce this week's character trait. This will include an optional team building exercise. If you have time you could do this as a Huddle. You might even suggest to your coach your whole team could do this outside of the Team Huddle. After this warm up you will have the opportunity to look into the ultimate source of character building—the Bible—and discover how it might guide you as you build your character.

What is a Team Huddle? A Team Huddle is a group of athletes from a team desiring to discuss real life and build their character through God's principles.

How big should a Team Huddle be? This is hard to say, but generally people feel most comfortable talking and learning in a group of 10 or fewer. The bottom line is that those on your team that want to be involved should have the chance, if it is only 3 or even if it is over 20.

When should we meet? Team Huddles typically meet during the team's season. The best time to do it is before or after practice, so you are not adding another time commitment to your already busy life.

What am I committing to by being a part of a Team Huddle? The best way to get something out of the Team Huddle is to make a commitment to it. To help you do that, we have developed a Team Huddle Commitment. It isn't complicated, but it is important that you take the time to read them at the end of this introduction and then sign the commitments.

How can I get the most out of this? You will get out of this exactly what you put into it. How honest you are with yourself and the others in the Huddle will determine how much you will get out of this. It might be a stretch for some of you to risk being vulnerable and honest for the first time.

Who can lead a Team Huddle? Team Huddles are best led by someone connected with your team! It could be a player, coach, assistant coach, chaplain, etc. It is not difficult to lead a Team Huddle. You don't have to be an expert in any particular area. You simply need to want to help teammates build their character. It is important that the Team Huddle leaders are aware of FCA's Statement of Faith and are in agreement with it.

FCA's Team Huddles Commitments

- Priority--As long as you are a part of the Team Huddle, you must make the meetings a priority.
- Participation--Everyone participates, no one dominates.
- Respect--Everyone is given the right to their own opinion, and all questions are encouraged and respected.
- Confidentiality--Anything that is said in the group stays in the group and is never repeated outside of the meeting.
- Empty Chair--The group remains open to new teammates.
- Support--Permission is given to call upon each other in times of need--even in the middle of the night.
- Giving Advice--Unsolicited advice is not allowed.
- Multiplication--We agree to do everything in our power to pray that others on your team would be interested in developing their character through God's principles.

DISCIPLINE

PROPERLY TRAINED

What did God teach you this week about character?

Except for the super heavyweight division, every wrestler or boxer steps on the scale prior to their match with the understanding that if they are overweight, they are immediately disqualified. Weeks and months of disciplining their body, could wasted before they ever compete.

Hamilton-Brown, a boxer from South Africa, suffered the consequences of an undisciplined lifestyle after his bout in the 1936 Olympics. Declared the loser in a split decision, Hamilton-Brown tried to ease his pain by going on an eating binge. Hours later, officials found a scoring error and gave him the victory. However, his lack of self-control had caused him to gain five pounds; therefore, he was over the weight limit. He was disqualified the following day!

Discipline: Receiving instruction and correction in a positive way; maintaining and enforcing proper conduct in accordance with the guidelines and rules.

1. What can you learn from the story of Hamilton-Brown?

2. Share a time when you experienced the benefits of a disciplined life choice.

Team Builder (optional): Have several members of your team share a time when they did something that was "stupid or idiotic" which could have been avoided if they had chosen to be disciplined. Use this Team Builder exercise to focus on the future, not on the past.

You have to love Shadrach, Meshach and Abednego (read Daniel 3:8-30). When it came to crunch time in their faith, they refused to bow down to the golden image that King Nebuchadnezzar built. They realized the consequences of their actions would result in being thrown into the fiery furnace. They knew God was more than capable of saving them from the fire, but even if He didn't, they would never compromise by worshipping anything or anyone besides the Lord. Though we know very little of the upbringing of these three young men prior to coming to Babylon, we can tell that they were disciplined men who had been properly trained from their youth. In their time of trial, they were prepared to meet this challenge.

Accepting and practicing discipline are two areas for us to consider. The first involves the discipline needed to help our team learn proper behaviors and actions. The second involves the results that occur when we become disciplined.

There are many times during the course of a sporting season when discipline is put into place.

Accepting discipline means understanding that the goals established by my team will not be reached unless we abide by the rules. If one of my teammates breaks the rules, we all suffer.

Accepting discipline leads to practicing discipline. One of the ways this occurs is by following the coaches' directives. Kim Oden was honored as the 1980's collegiate volleyball player of the decade for her contributions at Stanford and as a two-time Olympian, but early in her career she learned the importance of seeking guidance from her coaches. She said, "Lots of us have been playing volleyball a long time, and in tight situations we're thinking, 'We're the ones who are out on the court playing and you coaches are on the bench over there watching.' There's no way we're always going to think the same way as our coach. But a lot of times, following our will, especially if it doesn't work, will cause us to end up on the bench. It's not an easy choice to follow your coach when you know the result will be painful, like doing sprints or weights and repetitions, but those disciplines are definitely worth it." As a team becomes more disciplined, it puts it in a better position to succeed.

1. Discipline comes from God and is often administered through our parents or other people in authority. You cannot become an outstanding person without discipline in your life. Describe how your parents, teachers and coaches discipline(d) you? Do you feel that this is/was appropriate?

2. What should be our attitude toward discipline?

3. What are the keys to becoming disciplined?

WRAPUP

My high school football coach told me that if he ever stopped disciplining me it meant he had given up on me as a player. He was convinced I could play better and through tough standards, he achieved the results he was looking for. Though my parents loved me unconditionally, they also told me the same thing. They knew that discipline would equip me to be the person God had designed me to be. Discipline goes beyond punishment by encouraging the desire to never repeat misdeeds, but instead to make better choices. We are reminded in Scripture that the Lord loves those whom he disciplines (Hebrews 12:6-11). When disciplined, our response will either be one of acceptance and learning from the situation or we can become embittered or angry. A defensive reaction could be a tragic mistake. Therefore, each of us can learn tremendous lessons when we are willing to accept discipline. David Augsburger, "Life without confrontation (or discipline) is directionless, aimless, passive. When unchallenged, human beings tend to drift, to wander or to stagnate. Confrontation is a gift. Confrontation is a necessary stimulation to jog one out of mediocrity or to prod one back from extremes."

The process of accepting and practicing discipline causes us to become personally disciplined. A disciplined person is able to stand up on his or her own two feet, with rock solid judgment and wisdom. Men and women (and teams) who are disciplined are easily distinguished from those who are not. A high level of character and leadership qualities emerges. Others will follow a disciplined person because he or she is prepared to handle any situation.

1. Read Proverbs 3:11-12, 18; Proverbs 13:24; Proverbs 22:15; Revelations 3:19. What do these verses tell us about our attitude as we receive discipline? How does love relate to our Father's discipline of His children?

2. Would you describe yourself as a disciplined person? Why or why not?

3. How can you live a more disciplined life at home? At school? In your sport? On the job?

4. Read Hebrews 12:6-11. What are ways the Lord has disciplined you in the past in order to train you for the future?

5. How do you respond when you are disciplined by someone? Describe how you would like to be disciplined by those in authority in order to bring about your best response (how do you like to be disciplined, frequency of the discipline, where the discipline is administered, etc.).

This week, memorize...

"Whoever loves instruction loves knowledge, but one who hates correction is stupid." Proverbs 12:1

Lord, discipline comes from you and others to aid me in becoming an outstanding person. Help me to...

DISCRETION

BREAKING AWAY FROM TEMPTATION

Recite the Scripture verse from the last study. What did God teach you this week about character?

Police forces across America watch the NBA, NFL and MLB playoff games with deep personal interest. They are responsible for protecting citizens, and sometimes even themselves! Championship celebrations are famous for injury and destruction of property, but surely Chicago holds the record. After the Bulls won the 1993 championship, 3 people were killed, 20 shot, 197 businesses looted and 173 felony charges resulted from the mayhem. If it weren't for the police, who knows how much greater the carnage would have been. Obviously these celebrants didn't show good discretion.

Discretion: Recognizing and avoiding words, actions and attitudes which could result in undesirable consequences.

1. How would you describe "discretion?"

2. What are potential consequences when we do not show discretion?

Team Builder (Optional): Place everyone in groups of two or three. Assign each group one of the following Bible verses and answer the questions below. 1 Chronicles 22:12; Proverbs 2:11; Proverbs 5:1-2; Proverbs 11:22; and Proverbs 19:11.

Observation:
What does it say?
Interpretation:
What does it mean?
Application:
How do I respond?

The nation of Israel turned its back from the Lord. King after king led them into deeper corruption, farther and farther away from God. However, King Hezekiah was a breath of fresh air. The Scriptures tell us that he trusted in the Lord as he clung to Him. He removed the false gods and idols. He returned God's Word to the people. Guess what happened to Hezekiah and his people? The Scriptures tell us that they prospered under his reign (read 2 Kings 18:1-12).

God is eager to give a blessing to those who seek after him. One of the definitions of discretion is "power of free decision or latitude of choice." Hezekiah demonstrated discretion as he chose to break away from the temptations that had plagued the kings before him.

In Africa, monkeys are hunted for their meat. A crafty method is used to trap the animals by fastening large wooden vases to trees. Each vase has a single opening, just big enough for the outstretched hand of an adult monkey. Candy is put inside the vases because the smell lures the monkeys to reach inside. With candy clutched their doubled-up fists are too large to go back through the openings. Rather than let go of the candy to escape, most monkeys refuse to drop their treasures even when they see the hunters approach. They are trapped by their foolish greed. Clearly we are not stupid, foolish monkeys. Obviously, our attraction to inappropriate behaviors or substances which brings pleasure can be strong. Clear thinking can be overcome by our desires to be gratified. Our discretion can become lost as our minds become clouded. Our thinking was thwarted. But once we see the trap and know we are caught, we would be monkeys, indeed, if we kept hanging on to our candy.

Like monkeys, we are often caught in a trap. We falsely believe we can hang on to our "candy" and still be free. Yet, even when we recognize the trap, we continue to hang on. When we finally realize we cannot have it both ways we let go and let God have control. At last we find freedom.

1. Think of someone you know that demonstrates good discretion. Why did you select him/her?

2. What happens to us when we lack discretion? How can we maintain discretion?

3. What does using discretion mean to you in your school life? In your sport and on your team? At home? On the job?

4. How do my choice of words, actions and attitudes impact my entire team?

WRAPUP

God grants freedom for us to choose the path and direction of our lives. We are warned in Matthew 7:13-14 that the path to God is a narrow road, and only a few find it. Along the path of life there are many appealing lures to tempt us and pull us away from our relationship with God. But with discernment and a solid relationship with Christ, we will find the narrow road.

The reality is that each of us has weak spots where we are susceptible to the temptations of this world. Though some may fall due to one bad decision, most of those who get into trouble make a series of tiny bad decisions—even decisions that go undetected— that slowly wear down the character of a person. God's Word teaches us to stand firm in the faith and guard against falling away (Hebrews 5:14).

One of the best choices you can make is to become accountable to another person and potentially one of the best candidates may be a current teammate. Unfortunately, many fall away because they do not have to answer to anyone for their behavior. Being accountable is owning up to past hurts and present shortcomings by committing to positive change. It begins with seeing the need to make changes and courage to make it happen with a new plan of action. Every person needs protection from self, along with a safety net. Pride is the biggest enemy. We need to bring ourselves to a point where we can confess our sins one to another. By the way, did you know that King Hezekiah had an accountability partner? His identity is found in 2 Kings 19:5-6.

1. Discretion keeps us alert to potential dangers and sinful living. How well do you handle the temptations of this world? Are you satisfied with your response?

2. King Hezekiah had Isaiah as an accountability partner (or a teammate). Who is someone that does (or can do) this for you?

What is the main reason you resist accountability? What is the main reason you want accountability?

3. We gain discretion and save ourselves from many problems when we listen to and obey God's Word and our accountability partner(s). How do your friends rate? Are your friends drawing you closer to God and to His will for your life?

4. Is anyone in your life asking you hard questions about the real issues that you face on a daily basis? If there isn't someone, would you be interested in establishing this type of friendship? Why or why not?

OVERTIME

This week, memorize...

"Discretion will watch over you, and understanding will guard you..." Proverbs 2:11

Lord, I want to gain discretion and save myself from many problems. Help me to...

FAITHFULNESS

Recite the Scripture verse from the last study. What did God teach you this week about character?

Ron Brown had accepted that his coaching days were over until his phone rang in December 2007. Bo Pelini was on the other end. Brown hadn't heard from Pelini in four years, since both were assistants at Nebraska under Frank Solich. Shortly after Solich's firing, Pelini and Brown were also let go. When they parted, Pelini told Brown that if he ever became a head coach, he wanted Brown on his staff. That long-promised job offer came soon after Pelini's hiring at Nebraska. "I would never hold a guy to do that four years later," Brown said. "We hadn't been in contact really. He kept his word. There are a lot of people he could have hired. By the grace of God, I'm here."

Faithfulness: Being thorough in the performance of my duties; being true to my words, promises and vows.

1. What can you learn about faithfulness from the perspective of Bo Pelini and Ron Brown?

2. Share an example where faithfulness was demonstrated in your life and the results that ensued.

Team Builder (Optional): Start off your meeting with a discussion of faithfulness by answering questions such as: "What is it? How is it demonstrated on our team? When have we seen it?" After the discussion ends, vote on which team member is the most faithful by a secret ballot. Announce the winner at the end of the meeting.

Pelini said Brown's energy and enthusiasm are infectious and just what the Huskers need after losing seasons two of the past four years. "He represents so many great things about what we're trying to instill in our players, it was a no-brainer to hire him," Pelini said. "Him being out of coaching for however many years, it was crazy." Brown noted, "I had accepted that I would never coach again at the college level." But Pelini pursued him, just as he had said he would.

The book of Ruth tells about a family relationship that endured through hardships. The love and loyalty that led Ruth to stay with her mother-in-law (Naomi) when her husband died can be a model for our relationships. Though Ruth and Naomi were from different lands and families, Ruth insisted on staying, even though Naomi urged her to return to her people and find another husband (read Ruth 1:1-18). Ruth's loyalty to Naomi resulted in a joyous wedding with Boaz, but loyalty to friends and family is valuable even without a happy ending.

Sadly, the virtue of faithfulness is not easily found in the world today. When things are inconvenient or difficult circumstances arise, many people bail. Unfaithfulness seems to be the norm far too often. In considering faithfulness, Psalm 119:90 reminds us that God's faithfulness continues through all generations. Certainly God's faithfulness is something we can count on. The Psalms are filled with acknowledgments of God's faithfulness. He is absolutely trustworthy in all He has promised.

Loyalty and personal faith go together. Our faith is to be lived out every day of the week and in every action we take, every word we speak, and every relationship we make. It's meant to be an overflow of everything we say and do. The measure of a person is not what happens on Sunday at church, but rather who he is Monday through Saturday.

Faithfulness is just as critical in our actions. It is being so consistent in our character that people know how we will respond in tough situations. It is critical for our witness to others that we are beyond reproach in this area. Trust is at the heart of any good relationship—with God or with others. God has certainly held up His end of the relationship. Are you ready to hold up yours with your team this season?

1. Name someone who is faithful to you. Why did you select him/her?

2. Why do you think it is difficult to find faithful men and women?

3. Why is it easy to trust people who are faithful/loyal?

WRAPUP

Daniel Taylor reminds us of the values of faithfulness in our actions, not just words, when he said, "Character is not something you have; it is something you are that inevitably shows itself in what you do. It is determined by the stories of which you are a part. As the concept of character makes a highly visible comeback in our public conversation, we must rescue it from glib politicians, do-gooders, and busy-body moralizers." God is challenging us to pursue faithfulness regardless of the personal cost, the effort required, or the lack of resulting public acclaim.

The verse, "Let your 'Yes' be yes, and your 'No,' no" is at the heart of what it means to be faithful (James 5:12). A faithful person is a one who can be trusted for his or her word, work and actions. In Matthew 5:33-37, Jesus tells the disciples that they should be known so well for their integrity that they should never have to take an oath. The oaths of yesterday are the legal contracts of today. We can do almost nothing today without signing a legal contract. Fifty years ago a handshake was still considered binding, because people felt that keeping their word was important. But, today our word means nothing to anyone because of a general lack of societal integrity. Faithfulness is not just keeping your word, it is telling the truth. What you say must be true.

The habit of being faithful to our Lord provides clear guidance for daily living. A simple step of faithfulness gives us the confidence to take the next step. Although we may be tempted to say "yes" to something that may enhance our popularity, we faithfully choose to say "no" to anything that will compromise our intimacy with God. We trust that God's way is best. Faith enables us to give up what seems good on the surface and patiently wait for what is best.

1. Read Psalm 31:23; Proverbs 3:3-4; Proverbs 13:17; Proverbs 20:6; and Proverbs 28:20. What should be our attitude concerning faithfulness to God? What are the results of faithfulness? What does God promise to His faithful ones?

2. Would you describe yourself as being faithful in the following environments? Share examples.
- With your family
- At school
- To your friends
- On your team
- At church
- On your job

3. How do people build loyalty? How do you feel about those who are loyal to you?

4. Compare faithfulness and success. Do they always occur together? Why or why not?

This week, memorize...

"Don't be afraid of what you are about to suffer. Look, the Devil is about to throw some of you into prison to test you, and you will have tribulation for 10 days. Be faithful until death, and I will give you the crown of life" Revelation 2:10

This week, I want to express faithfulness to God and others. Help me to....

FEAR OF THE LORD

EXPERIENCING AN EARTHQUAKE

Recite the Scripture verse from the last study. What did God teach you this week about character?

Rosalynn Sumners won a silver medal in figure skating in the 1984 Winter Olympics. While on the outside she appeared to have everything—money, fame, popularity and excitement—Rosalyn had deep internal struggles. She battled loneliness on the road, and she felt tremendous pressure to perform day after day. She reflects, "I realize how fortunate I am to be a professional figure skater but the glamour, money and fame weren't giving me a sense of purpose. I had unmet needs that went deeper than my Olympic experiences and career." Several years ago, Rosalynn discovered what was missing—a personal relationship with Jesus Christ. She now has the fear of the Lord in her life and it

has brought great peace and contentment. She said, "Jesus Christ is the only person I can be completely vulnerable, raw and honest with."

Fear of the Lord: Having a sense of awe and respect for Almighty God which goes above and beyond anyone or anything else.

1. Have you ever experienced life or felt the thoughts expressed by Rosalynn?

2. Discuss her situation compared to your own life. How did you react to her final statement?

Team Builder (Optional): Has anyone experienced a hurricane or other natural disaster? Describe to the group a few of the details and the emotions involved. Have several members share their stories and note any similarities.

To fear the Lord means to maintain a healthy respect for Almighty God. Some people have a problem respecting both God and man's human authority. Earl Cochell seemed to have such a problem with an explosion of words which some would describe as an "earthquake tremor." The hot-headed tennis pro saw his career come to an abrupt end when he stormed the umpire's chair to gain control of the microphone in an attempt to cuss out the crowd at the US Nationals.

Scientists say that between 2,500 and 10,000 small earthquakes ripple our planet every day. Most are minor tremors, but many remember the October 17, 1989 quake that interrupted the World Series in San Francisco. An even bigger quake hit southern Missouri in 1812 and changed the course of the Mississippi River. These tremors shake our confidence in the very ground we walk on and bring fear to the hearts of men. My wife and I experienced our first earthquake together while on the 24th floor in a San Diego hotel. We awoke from a deep sleep in the middle of the night to a swaying and creaking building. Like many in the hotel, we were frightened.

Jonah had an "earthquake type" experience when he tried running from God after the Lord told him to go to Ninevah. But God got his attention and imparted the fear of the Lord in him when a huge fish swallowed him and took him on a three-day voyage. When Jonah was spit out of the whale, he was willing to go to Ninevah and proclaim God's message (read Jonah 1:1-17 and 3:1-2).

One of the healthiest motivators we can have in our lives is the recognition of a "fear of the Lord" above and beyond fearing anyone or anything else. The fear of the Lord gives you a new attitude—an attitude that brings about practical application of God's commands and principles. A fear of man responds to the pleasures of people because they're afraid of what others will think. To fear the Lord means to maintain a healthy reverent respect and awe for Almighty God. When you fear the Lord, you're obedient to Him regardless of the cost or the audience. When we have this type of perspective, we are able to perform solely for the Lord and not for others as noted in Colossians 3:17-24.

1. What is something that you fear? Why do you fear it?

2. Describe how you picture God. What has helped shape your views about God?

3. How does your response in #1 and #2 (above) compare with your "fear of the Lord?"

God expects our best effort in all of our endeavors. Whether on the job, in the classroom, on the athletic field, within our church or with our family, we are supposed to do our best for God's glory. He is the one we serve, as we fear and honor Him.

To fear God means we need not fear anything or anyone else in this world. We should be more concerned with what God thinks than what people think. Yet this can be difficult because we can be easily become fearful—fear of failure, fear of rejection, fear of the past, fear of guilt, fear of embarrassment, fear of loneliness, fear of personal relationships, fear of being hurt, fear of accidents. Whatever terror haunts us can lead to a life filled with fear.

When we think that God cannot or will not help us, we leave ourselves wide open to these fears. However, when we are convinced that God's power is greater than any evil that could come upon us; we can live with confidence and hope. While fear paralyzes us, a healthy "fear of the Lord" helps us to think clearly, see real danger, and take reasonable risks.

We can place our confidence in God's hands and agree with Paul when he said, "And we know that in all things God works for the good of those who love him, who have been called according to his purpose" (Romans 8:28). What is God's purpose? Is it not that we should love him and trust him? Love and trust make no room for fear. So, listen to Jesus, when he tells us, "Do not be afraid ... I am with you always" (Matthew 28:10, 20).

1. Read Proverbs 1:7; 8:13; 10:27; 14:26-27; and 19:23. How important is the fear of the Lord? According to Scripture, what are the results of fearing God? Read Proverbs 2:1-5. How do we learn the fear of the Lord?

2. What does a healthy perspective of "fearing the Lord" involve for each of us as individuals? How can this character quality impact our team as a whole?

3. God views disobedience very seriously. Read 2 Samuel 6:1-7 and what occurred to Uzzah when he didn't follow God's commands as stated in Numbers 4:15. What can you learn from this incident as it relates to Uzzah and "fear of the Lord?"

4. A wise person fears the Lord and shuns evil (Proverbs 14:16). Do you have a "fear of the Lord?" How do you live this out?

This week, memorize...

"Happy is the one who is always reverent, but one who hardens his heart falls into trouble" Proverbs 28:14

Lord, I commit to maintain a proper perspective of "fear" and a "fear of the Lord". Help me to....

HONESTY

Recite the Scripture verse from the last study. What did God teach you this week about character?

In the 1990 qualifying school for the PGA Tour, golfer Tom Lehman called a penalty on himself when he noticed a strong breeze caused his ball to move slightly as he addressed it. He wound up missing the cut by one stroke. "If a breach of the rules had occurred and I didn't call it on myself, I couldn't look at myself in the mirror," he responded. "You're only as good as your word. And your word wouldn't be worth much if you can't even be honest with yourself."

In contrast to Lehman's honesty, Olympic sprinter Marion Jones lied for years about her use of steroids and other performance enhancing drugs. Her lack of honesty landed her in prison.

Honesty: Proclaiming the truth with sincerity and frankness in all situations.

1. What can we learn from these two stories related to the importance of honesty?

2. Share a time when you saw honesty demonstrated and the results of this act.

Team Builder (Optional): Before your meeting, do a "google" search on honest and dishonest athletes. Bring your findings to the meeting and discuss the benefits and consequences of honesty in athletics. Did you find any examples when dishonesty pays off? How about honesty?

Disgraced American Olympic hero Marion Jones went to prison for lying to law enforcement officials about using steroids and a check-fraud scheme. "I made a mistake," she stated. "I made a choice, at the time, to protect myself, to protect my family. And now I've paid the consequences dearly." Jones said she hopes others will learn from her missteps. "I want people to understand that, you know, everybody makes mistakes. I truly think that a person's character is determined by their admission of their mistakes and then beyond that, what do I do about it?"

Jones' tearful confession to doping after years of denials was followed by Jones returning the three gold medals and two bronze medals she won at the 2000 Sydney Olympics. Jones captured gold in the 100- and meters and helped the 4x100 relay to gold as well. She was also a five-time world champion. But now, Jones has had all results since September 1, 2000, stricken from the records and has been banned from future competition. Jones lied to federal agents three times, starting in November of 2003 when asked about her connections to the BALCO steroid scandal.

Jones' admission not only resulted in the return of her medals, but it also cost her three teammates on the relay team their medals as well. USOC Olympic chairman Peter Ueberroth said the relays were tainted because of Jones' presence and thus all the medals were returned. These innocent teammates were deeply affected by Jones' dishonesty.

I'll admit that there have been times when I have been dishonest. With full knowledge, I've tweaked stories and told outright, boldfaced lies. It's hard to look people in the eye trying to maintain integrity while sharing false facts. The trouble intensifies when the lie begins to perpetuate itself into other conversations. As the lie progresses to other people, do I now come clean or does the lie continue? Who knows the truth and who has heard the lie? The mental deception that goes on in our minds can literally destroy us.

Dishonesty not only eats us up but as you can see from Marion Jones' story, it can also have a devastating impact on our entire team. It has been said, "The truth wins in the end. Therefore, make friends with the truth. If we are honest, truth is our best friend. If we are dishonest, truth is our greatest enemy."

1. Who is the most honest person you know? Why did you select him/her?

2. Is it ever right to lie? Explain your answer.

3. What are the results of honesty? What are the results of dishonesty?

WRAPUP

What in the world were Ananias and Sapphira thinking? In Acts 4:32-35, the believers were willingly sharing among themselves. There was evidence of great power and provision. It was a joyous time for everyone. But this couple decided not to follow the leadership of the church and they outright lied to Peter about the proceeds of their property sale. Their dishonesty resulted in immediate death.

Dishonesty may not bring immediate physical death like we see from Ananias and Sapphira, but certainly death occurs mentally, intellectually, emotionally and spiritually.

Honesty breeds life while dishonesty breeds death. Situations and life itself get very complicated and confusing when the truth is not shared.

Jesus told us that the "truth will set us free." What a liberating promise from God that the truth is always the best policy no matter how inconvenient it may seem. Even if complete honesty brings temporary pain, God will honor your courage and bless you for doing the right thing. I'll admit it takes courage to be honest. Be reminded that you will please the Lord when you speak the truth, admit when you are wrong and not rationalize or minimize your inappropriate words or actions. Knowing we have the support and friendship of God and others supplies the courage we may lack.

There's also another benefit to honesty as seen in the response of former Speaker of the House Sam Rayburn when asked a question by a reporter many years ago, "Mr. Speaker, you see at least a hundred people a day. You tell each one yes or no. You never seem to take notes on what you've told them, but I've never heard of you forgetting anything you have promised them. What is your secret? Rayburn's eyes flashed as he answered, "If you tell the truth the first time, you don't have anything to remember."

1. Read the following verses from Proverbs—12:22; 14:5; 14:25; 19:5; 21:28 and 26:28. From these verses contrast the truthful man versus the liar. What is God's perspective on honesty?

2. Share a time where you experienced "the truth setting you free." Why are Jesus' words true?

3. What are the benefits of being a person committed to telling the truth?

4. Your name is tied to your character. If your character is dishonest, so will be your name. A reputation of having a good name and being honest will follow you and your children all the days of your life. How does being honest today impact you and your legacy?

This week, memorize...

"Righteous lips are a king's delight, and he loves one who speaks honestly." Proverbs 16:13

Lord, an honest response pleases you and allows me to experience freedom. Help me to....

HOPE

PLACE YOUR TRUST IN HIM

Recite the Scripture verse from the last study. What did God teach you this week about character?

Tailback Otis Mounds had no hope of getting into the game as a freshman at Auburn University. Otis had suffered a hamstring injury, and coach Pat Dye planned to redshirt him. So he attended Auburn's 1990 home opener against Fullerton State as a fan. Mounds cheered Auburn's first touchdown and thought nothing of it when the starting tailback left the game with an ankle injury. When the second-string tailback was injured in the second quarter, he started to wonder what the coach would do. Amazingly, as Otis watched the half-time show from the upper deck, the public's address announcer said: "Will Otis Mounds please report to the Auburn locker room?" Sprinting through the crowd, he found

Coach Dye waiting with a jersey. His hopes were rekindled, and by the end of the game Otis Mounds had carried the ball five times for 33 yards in a 38-17 victory! Not bad for a guy who had no hope of playing when the game began.

Hope: Feeling that my deepest desire will be realized and that events will turn out for the best.

1. Tell a time where you were in a hopeless situation and miraculously things changed, which brought about hope.

Team Builder (Optional): As a team, come up with some creative ways to give hope to someone in need around your school. Once you have come up with some great ideas put those ideas into action by doing this for a student, teacher, coach, staff member, booster club volunteer or one of the parents within the next week.

Have you ever seen a team become demoralized in the midst of a game? When this happens, the sideline becomes eerily silent with heads downcast. Spirits sag as the team loses hope in their quest to be victorious. When this occurs, it is a near impossibility to reverse the outcome. It is important in these moments for the team members to realize that the scoreboard should not be the primary goal. The ultimate goal is to maintain a focus on the Lord and His calling.

Bethany Hamilton was once ranked as the best amateur teen surfer in Hawaii. In October 2003, however, she lost one of her arms to a tiger shark while surfing. The story of a beautiful and talented teenager losing an arm to a shark made national news. As the world watched the story unfold it saw Bethany display something that kept her from being depressed and sinking into a life of self-pity. She had a relationship with Jesus Christ, and that transcended the tragedy she experienced.

Soon after the attack, Bethany began to raise money to restore a man's eyesight. While she was visiting New York City, she gave her ski coat to a homeless girl. Her story appeared in a national newspaper stating: "As always, Hamilton remains undaunted. She has told her father that if having only one arm proved detrimental to reaching the top in competitive surfing, then she'd see about playing soccer." Her pastor said, "She's looking forward to the future. She's asking herself, 'How can I show the world I still have a life, that I enjoy my life, and that my life is filled with joy?' She has an underlying trust that God is taking care of her."

The key to Bethany's attitude is she understands who she is, whose she is and where she is. Because of her understanding of those three basic truths she is able to turn tragedy into triumph. It is all because of the fact that Bethany's heart has been enlightened to know "the hope of His calling."

Do you have the same kind of hope that Bethany has? It can only be found by surrendering your heart and life totally to Jesus as your Savior and Lord. Don't wait . . . surrender to Him right now and begin a life of hope and purpose!

1. Name someone who has hope in his/her life. Why did you select this person?

2. The pessimist sees the difficulty in every opportunity and the optimist sees the opportunity in every difficulty. Would you describe yourself as optimistic or pessimistic? Why?

3. How do you feel when a longing is fulfilled? In contrast, how do you feel when hope is shattered?

WRAPUP

Someone wisely said, "You can live forty days without food, five days without water and five minutes without air...but you can't live one second without hope." The army of Israel had lost all hope while in battle against the Philistines. Goliath daily taunted them, driving them further into despair. When David arrived on the scene, he was appalled at the attitude of his brothers and King Saul. David had hope in the Lord, which gave him courage to take on the great giant. He proclaims in 1 Samuel 17:45-47 that God would be victorious and what David believed happened. When confronted with a Goliath-sized problem, which way do you respond: "He's too big to hit," or like David, "He's too big to miss." The entire story of David and Goliath as noted in 1 Samuel 17 is a good lesson for any team to consider...especially for a team which believes they are in a hopeless situation.

God is good to us. He restores hope in hopeless situations and it is He who gives hope as we face the future. While some put their hope in visible and tangible things, God tells us to place our hope and trust in Him alone.

Everything that occurs has been sifted through the Father's hands before it reaches us. He's in total and complete control. When you're in the middle of a crisis, where is your hope?

1. Read the following Scripture verses: Psalm 39:7; Proverbs 10:28, 13:19; 24:14; 24:20; 26:12. What do these verses tell us about hope and hopelessness? What ultimately happens to the hopeless?

2. Describe a time when you or your team had no hope. Where did you or your team turn for help? What was the ultimate result?

3. Where do you turn to receive hope?

4. Romans 10:11 tells us that whoever trusts in the Lord will not be disappointed. Do you believe this verse? Why or why not? Go on a Bible search to look for additional passages which remind us that God is our hope.

5. Discuss the following comment: "A lack of hope has killed more splendid projects, shattered more ambitious schemes, strangled more effective geniuses, neutralized more superb efforts, blasted more fine intellects, and thwarted more worthy ambitions than any other enemy of the human race."

OVERTIME

This week, memorize...

"Delayed hope makes the heart sick, but fulfilled desire is a tree of life." Proverbs 13:12

Lord, I will place my hope in you and you alone. Help me to...

KINDNESS

GETTING YOUR EYES OFF OF SELF

Recite the Scripture verse from the last study. What did God teach you this week about character?

Sara Tucholsky of Western Oregon University uncorked her first home run in her college career with two runners on base in a playoff game against Central Washington University. While rounding the bases, she missed first base. As she started back to tag it, she collapsed with a knee injury. She was only able to crawl back to first but could do no more. She would been called out if her own teammates had helped her around the bases.

Central Washington first baseman Mallory Holtman, asked the umpire if she and her teammates could help Tucholsky. The umpire said there was no rule against it.

So Holtman and shortstop Liz Wallace put their arms under Tucholsky's legs, and she put her arms over their shoulders. The three headed around the base paths, stopping to let Tucholsky touch each base with her good leg.

See the rest of her story in the WARMUP.

Kindness: Demonstrating a gentle, sympathetic attitude towards others.

1. Why is it important to be kind?

Team Builder (Optional): Supply everyone with a blank sheet of paper at the beginning of the meeting. Have everyone write a note of kindness expressing thankfulness for something they have done. Be specific by citing a certain time and place that a statement or act of kindness was displayed. At the end of the meeting have everyone mail or deliver the note to the person they wrote to.

"The only thing I remember is that Mallory asked me which leg was the one that hurt," Tucholsky said. "I told her it was my right leg and she said, 'OK, we're going to drop you down gently and you need to touch it with your left leg.'"

"We started laughing when we touched second base," Holtman said. "I said, 'I wonder what this must look like to other people.'"

"We didn't know that she was a senior or that this was her first home run," Wallace said. "That makes the story more touching than it was. We just wanted to help her." Holtman said she and Wallace weren't thinking about the playoff spot, and didn't consider the gesture something special. "I hope I would do the same for her in the same situation," Tucholsky added. As the trio reached home plate, the entire Western Oregon team was in tears.

"In the end, it is not about winning and losing so much," Holtman said. "It was about this girl. She hit it over the fence and was in pain, and she deserved a home run."

The parable of the Good Samaritan illustrates kindness to a high degree. While the religious elite ignored the beaten man on the side of the road, the Samaritan felt compassion. In those days, Samaritans were despised, lowly people. It would've been well within the rights of the Samaritan to simply reciprocate evil for evil, but instead he chose to be kind. After bandaging his wounds, he carried the beaten man to an inn where he could safely recover. He also personally paid the innkeeper and promised to return later in case more money was needed for the beaten man's care. This act of kindness is a model of unselfishness.

We live in a society where we are consumed with, "me, myself and I." We're so busy taking care of ourselves and our agendas that we miss out on daily opportunities to bless and encourage others through acts of kindness. The Good Samaritan's story is rare because he put the needs of someone else above his own. He saw a need, he reached out to help and he was honestly concerned. He did more than just think about doing something, he responded. Though we don't know the end of the story, we can assume that when the beaten man recovered he probably was more gentle and kind than before because of the care he received. Kindness is important to God because He sees every deed and hears every thought and word.

1. Who do you know that is kind? Why did you think of him/her?

2. Sara Tucholsky has seen the value of kindness even in the midst of competition. Have you ever experienced or demonstrated unusual kindness in competition? What was the result of this kind act?

3. How do we get away from the "me, myself and I" mentality and begin to focus on others?

WRAPUP

Showing kindness is important to God because He sees every deed and hears every thought and word. Kindness can take on many different forms. It may involve getting your hands dirty as you assist someone with a task. It may be quietly listening to someone who needs your ear. It might be volunteering your time or giving money to a needy organization. Kindness also includes good manners. It makes other people feel good about themselves, which often causes them to extend kindness and generosity they might not otherwise exhibit. There are even times that an act of kindness may be anonymous— that way God gets the credit. My good friend Don Hilkemeier used to say, "I'm going to do something nice for someone, and if they find out, it doesn't count." The key to kindness is getting your eyes off of yourself and putting them on others. It doesn't cost anything to be kind, but kindness can pay off in big ways.

Have you ever heard the phrase: "Kill them with kindness?" It means no matter how you are treated by someone, you are committed to being kind no matter how they respond. This occurred with one young athlete who despised a teammate. She went to her coach and shared, "I hate this person. She is making my life miserable. I want to make things as tough as possible for her. What do you advise?" The coach

replied, "Begin by showering her with compliments. Give until it hurts. That will tear her up." A few months later, the coach asked the girl, "Are you following my advice?" "I am," she answered, "and today she's one of my best friends."

Real kindness begins with action rather than ideas. Wisdom teaches us that you can act your way into a new way of thinking better than think your way into a new way of acting. We do the right thing first, regardless of our feelings and allow our feelings to catch up later. Great men and women have become great by simply exhibiting kindness.

1. Read the following verses: Proverbs 3:3; Proverbs 19:17; Proverbs 25:21-22; Romans 2:4 and Colossians 3:12. What do these passages tell us about our necessary behavior towards one another? What happens when we are kind?

2. Scripture tells us that God will reward our kindness one day. How can you be more kind at home? At school? In sports? On the job?

3. Comment on these two statements: "It's nice to be important, but it's more important to be nice" and "People don't care how much you know, until they know how much you care...about them." What can we learn from this type of attitude?

4. It's good to be a Christian and know it, but it's better to be a Christian and show it. Choose someone to whom you could show kindness. Make it your prayer and give your best effort to do it in the next few days.

This week, memorize...

"And be kind and compassionate to one another, forgiving one another, just as God also forgave you in Christ." Ephesians 4:32

Lord, I will exhibit kindness to my friends and my enemies. Help me to...

LOVE

THE POWER OF LOVE

Recite the Scripture verse from the last study. What did God teach you this week about character?

Ben Comen's lifetime dream was to be part of a team but no team wanted him, except for maybe being a water boy because Ben had cerebral palsy, a condition which affected his balance. Coach Parker willingly agreed to let Ben be part of the squad. Ben gave his all, knowing that he would finish last in virtually every race.

"I've been coaching cross-country for 31 years," says Coach Parker, "and I've never met anyone with Ben's drive." Coach Parker's team rallied behind Ben because of his incredible attitude. Their love for him was evidenced by the fact that his team and other competitors, after finishing their race, would backtrack to where Ben was at on the course, and run with him through the finish line again. While they were exhausted from their race, it was worth it for them to help Ben finish his race.

Love: Having a deep personal attachment and affection for another person.

1. Share a time when you had someone love you beyond what you could dream or imagine. How did this make you feel?

Team Builder (Optional): In this lesson we will be discussing the "Five Love Languages." Write the five love languages on the board for a quick reference. Before doing the lesson, have each team member write on a piece of paper the love language they believe they most often respond to. Have the rest of the team guess the individual answers. At the end of this lesson, see how closely you predicted the right answers.

Johnny and Marty were childhood friends from Atlanta who loved baseball and made a pact to always play together—no matter what happened. Johnny became the star of his team, while Marty struggled. One day their coach told Johnny about a minor league tryout. Johnny signed up right and he insisted on including Marty in the tryout to stand by his pact. He said, "I believe in Marty. We're friends. Believing in someone is the best kind of love."

At the tryout, both Johnny and Marty gave it their best effort. Johnny received a contract offer, but Marty was cut. "Leave your buddy. You've got great natural talent and potential," said the minor league coach. "It's both of us or neither of us," replied Johnny, and he left. Such loyalty and love was rare, and several days later both boys were awarded contracts. Marty became deeply inspired and began to improve. During their third year in the minors, Johnny Echols quit. Marty was called up by the St. Louis Cardinals to play shortstop. He became the team leader of the dynasty known as the GasHouse Gang of the 1940s. When they won the 1944 World Series, Marty Marion was named the MVP.

Jesus had a very special love for Mary, Martha and Lazarus. Luke 10:38-42 and John 11:1-45 gives insight into their relationship. Mary was often described as a "worshipper" while Martha was a "worker." When Lazarus died, Jesus wept. We see Mary's and Martha's unique personalities emerge in response to his death. In spite of their differences, we see that Jesus loved them equally.

Real love comes from God, who is love. Romans 5:8 tells us God demonstrated his own love for us in that while we were yet sinners, Christ died for us. This type of love is difficult to comprehend. Jesus also commanded us to love one another. Love has the power to believe in someone and to draw out the best in him or her. Love is being "other" oriented as defined in Philippians 2:3-4 and John 13:35. Giving love, rather than receiving love, is the goal. Self-gratification is not love. Love has to be freely and unconditionally given away. Eric Fromm described it this way, "Love means to commit oneself without guarantee; to give oneself completely in the hope that our love will live in the loved person. Love is an act of faith, and whoever is of little faith is also of little love."

1. Give an example of one who loves others. Why did you select him/her?

2. How do we love in a practical way?

3. Read 1 Corinthians 13 which is often referred to as the "love chapter." Since God is referred to in the Bible as the very essence of love, these verses remind us of God's great love for all people. How has God shown His love to you?

WRAPUP

The good news of the gospel of Christ is the same joyous message, loud and clear: God loves you! This is the indisputable fact of all life! It doesn't matter how good (or bad) you are at sports, God is love. If you have all A's or all F's, God is love. No matter how or why things fall apart we are still loved, and God is with us and available every second. Maybe we fail to call, or misdial, or give up too soon, or maybe we don't hear or don't like God's answer. God's grace works in ways beyond our understanding and quite often far exceeds our puny plans. Perhaps we can learn to accept His amazing plan even in the midst of chaos and pain.

One way to show love in a practical way can be discovered in Gary Chapman's book, *Five Languages of Love.* He states that one of the keys to successfully loving people is to understand one another's primary love language. The five love languages include: (1) words of affirmation, (2) gifts, (3) acts of service, (4) quality time and (5) physical touch. Each person has one love language, which means more to him/her than all the others. You may appreciate them all, but one will speak to you more deeply. If you can determine the love languages for each person important to you, it will help draw out deeper and more meaningful conversations. It will also solidify your love for one another.

1. Read Proverbs 10:12; Proverbs 15:17; Proverbs 17:17; John 3:16; 1 John 3:16 and 1 John 4:7-21. According to God's Word, what are the characteristics of love? Why is love such an important part of Christianity? Why does the Church believe, "they will know we are Christians by our love?"

2. How do you show love in your family? At school/job? In sports? To your teammates?

3. What relationship(s) do you need to strengthen by demonstrating more love in that relationship? What do you specifically need to do in this relationship?

4. When we love others by our deeds we are revealing that we know Him. Those who receive your love today will be more interested in hearing about your faith tomorrow. Discuss practical ways that you could be more loving to people.

5. Which of the five love languages means the most to you? How well did you predict the love language of your teammates, closest friends and family members? Compare and discuss your results.

This week, memorize...

"Dear friends, let us love one another, because love is from God, and everyone who loves has been born of God and knows God. The one who does not love does not know God, because God is love." 1 John 4:7-8

Lord, I will show my love for God and others. Help me to....

PEACEFUL

Recite the Scripture verse from the last study. What did God teach you this week about character?

Pat Manson, a former U.S. pole vault champion, loves Philippians 4:6-7. Pat reflects, "I love it when the Bible says things like do not be anxious about anything. Absolutes like the word "anything" is challenging. I find myself saying, 'But wait a second, this is really important. How can I not be anxious about this?' It's easy in Olympic level athletics to get really nervous about things. But the Bible says, 'No, do not be anxious.'" Six weeks before the Olympic Trials, Pat pulled a hamstring, jeopardizing his chance at making the U.S. team. He recalled the verse from Philippians and reminded himself not to be anxious, but to instead pray and petition the Lord with a thankful attitude.

Manson reminds us that we serve a wonderful, loving God who is on our side and offers incredible foundational security. He says, "Life is a great adventure. Sometimes there are bumps along the way, but He is always with us and truly offers peace that transcends understanding." The peace of God enabled Pat to relax and vault his best.

Peaceful: Being at rest with myself and others.

1. Pat was able to experience peace by focusing on God's truth. Where do you go and what do you do to find peace?

Team Builder (Optional): Schedule a "quiet moment" for your team (minimum 10 minutes) where no one is allowed to talk. During this time of reflection, seek God's peace. Afterwards discuss how this time made you feel.

The inner peace from God is available to all believers in spite of the turmoil in the world. Peter and Paul in Acts 12 and 16, respectively, both had peace while sitting in jail awaiting their fate. Peter had so much peace in his situation that he fell into a deep sleep. Paul was busy singing and praying when he was delivered. Both were neither worried nor anxious about the future.

Michelle Akers, one of the great all-time women's soccer players, said, "The more time I spend keeping my eye on who God is, His perspective, His goals for me, the more fun I have, the more joyful I feel, the more peace I have." Michelle is right...true peace only comes when you keep your eyes focused on God and not the problems and issues that confront you. What a feeling to have the freedom in releasing your burdens to Christ (read Matthew 11:28-30).

In our modern, fast paced world it's hard to find peace. One of the reasons is it's difficult being quiet. Stillness is something we rarely encounter. Think about it! Noise (music, television, talk, laughter, machinery, appliances, phones and traffic) from 6:00 am until midnight. Speed (bumper to bumper at 65 m.p.h., on-ramps and off-ramps, deadlines and appointments) causes us to check our watches more than checking in with the Lord. Activities (meetings, services, dinners, luncheons, breakfasts, rallies, clubs and sports) pull us away from quietness.

Our society is known for its busyness and in fact it has been called "the age of sprinting, squinting, and shoving." Everyone is in a hurry. Jesus calls us to follow Him in action but also to inaction—to literally "rest a while." God created rest in creation. In fact, God himself rested on the seventh day and made rest and relaxation itself holy.

When is the last time you've gotten quiet before the Lord and allowed His peace to overwhelm you? These quiet moments are when you can hear and feel the peaceful presence of God (Psalm 46:10). Then rely upon Him daily for peace and direction. Let Him be your refuge and strength.

1. Who do you know that most often demonstrates the peace of God?

2. On a scale of 1-10 (1-Anxious/Worried to 10-Totally at Peace), where would you describe yourself normally? Tell why you selected this number.

3. Where is your favorite place to be quiet? How do you feel when you are there?

WRAPUP

I commonly hear coaches and athletes asking the Lord to give them peace in the midst of highly competitive situations. Recently, I heard one coach remind his team to "enjoy the journey." He was trying to communicate that the stress of a season can result in lots of frustrations and disappointments. He admonished his team to seek God's peace and to ask Him to remove the anxiety and to have fun just playing the game. In the following weeks, his team responded to his peace challenge, and they performed better.

Most people have trouble resting, relaxing, and seeking contentment in solitude. We tend to soothe ourselves with people, activity, and noise. Yet we are also meant "to be still." Jesus invited his disciples, "Come away by yourselves to a lonely place and rest a while. For many were coming and going, and they had no leisure even to eat" (Mark 6:31). The way we "grab a bite" and "eat on the run," it is no wonder we have stomach problems.

In every situation, God knows more about what's involved than we can ever know. He alone sees the beginning and the ending. He alone knows how to create a master plan that provides for the good of those who serve Him. Only God knows what lies ahead for your life. It has been said, "We must experience peace with God before we can know the peace of God." True peace can only come as we place our hope in Him and trust His plans for our life.

It has been said, "If the devil can't make you bad, he'll make you busy." Life can be hectic. Thus, we need a place and a time where we can be renewed, refreshed and re-energized.

Let me suggest three critical things you may need to consider in becoming a person of peace: (1) Find a SANCTUARY -- A place you can get alone with God. It could be in a car, in a park or sitting in the school bleachers. It needs to be a place of solitude and silence where you can be still before God. (2) Honor the SABBATH -- set aside one day as a day of rest. While it may not be practical to do it every week, take active steps toward this happening and watch what it does to you. (3) Pursue SIMPLICITY -- You can't do it all. Remember, Jesus didn't do it all either. Establish priorities and pursue them vigorously. Say "no" to everything else.

1. Read Psalm 37:37; Proverbs 12:20; Proverbs 20:3; Romans 5:1; and Ephesians 2:14. Discuss the truths from these above verses on peace. Which verse(s) impact you? How do you obtain peace with God?

2. Are you experiencing God's peace in your heart? Why or why not?

3. How often do you get quiet before the Lord? Where do you go? How often do you do this? Are you satisfied with the amount of quietness you have?

This week, memorize...

"Abundant peace belongs to those who love Your instruction; nothing makes them stumble." Psalm 119:165

Lord, I will not be anxious. Instead I will seek God's peace. Help me to....

PRAYERFUL

Recite the Scripture verse from the last study. What did God teach you this week about character?

Danny Wuerffel was the 1996 Heisman Trophy winner while at the University of Florida, and he played quarterback in the NFL with a number of different teams before retiring in 2002. In his career, he has had a dynamic relationship with teammates and coaches due to his faith in God. Danny has a strong desire to wait upon the Lord through fellowship and prayer. He sensed the Lord's call to a greater devotion to prayer as noted later in the WARMUP.

Prayerful: Communing with God spiritually through adoration, confession, thanksgiving and supplication.

1. How active is your personal prayer life? Are you satisfied with it? Why or why not?

2. What could you do to enhance your prayer life?

Team Builder (Optional): Invite your team to participate in an extended prayer meeting where the only thing on the agenda is to pray for the team and the various needs voiced by team members. Discover how it will positively impact your team.

Danny Wuerffel shared, "I'm called to spend more time praying for myself, my family and others. I think sometimes we do so many Bible studies and go to so many churches and hear so many sermons, and it all goes to our head, but we don't take time to let it go to our hearts. That's why we need more private time with the Lord in prayer. The Lord is always talking; the question is whether we are listening. The most repeated phrase in the Old Testament is to 'call upon the name of the Lord.' I've been going through the Lord's prayer phrase by phrase trying to understand exactly what He meant by each word, trying to learn what it really means to call upon the name of the Lord. We must spend more time in prayer."

The demands of being an athlete or coach can be overwhelming. Even the best athletes are at risk of hitting rock bottom at some point. As Christians we are called to help get those who are going through hard times. This includes praying—praying for teammates who are struggling mentally or physically, praying for coaches who are in challenging situations, praying for wisdom and joy for you. As we pray for our fellow athletes and coaches, let's remember 1 John 5:14. "Now this is the confidence we have before Him: whenever we ask anything according to His will, He hears us."

The briefest biography in the entire Bible is buried in 1 Chronicles. The first nine chapters of this book contain the official family tree of the Hebrew tribes beginning with Adam and proceeding through thousands of years to Israel's return from captivity. The long lists of unfamiliar and difficult names— more than five hundred of them— are likely to bore even the most zealous Bible readers. When the writer gets to Jabez he pauses to share two brief verses with us. Jabez gives a simple, direct request to God. He trusted and believed that God would hear him. His prayer changed his entire life and left a permanent mark on the history.

William Carey said, "Prayer— secret, fervent, believing prayer— lies at the root of all personal godliness." Prayer is the central avenue that God uses to transform us.

1. Who is someone you know that has an active prayer life? How do you know this?

2. Do you believe in the power of prayer? Why or why not?

3. How has prayer impacted you personally?

4. Comment on the following: "When we depend on man, we get what man can do; when we depend on prayer, we get what God can do."

WRAPUP

Sometimes Christians are guilty of not asking God for enough. We settle for second best when we could be enjoying the fullness of His Spirit in every part of our lives. God tells us we are always to be asking, seeking and knocking on His door in prayer. Why is prayer important, and does it really make a difference? There is a recurring theme throughout Scripture: Prayer on earth results in action in heaven. One of the best examples of this is found in Revelations 8:1-5. In verse 1, we are told that there was silence for about half an hour. In the verses that follow we are told that it became quiet because of a prayer.

You see, when someone prays, God listens. God is attentive and carefully listening to our every word. Yes, prayer on earth results in action in heaven.

God hears the prayers of the humble, contrite soul as noted in Psalm 51:17. He desires for us to present our needs and cares before Him, but also with purity and brokenness. Psalm 66:18-20 reminds us that if we cherish sin in our hearts, clinging to any known practice, the Lord will not hear us. We must enter His presence clean. God hears the sincere prayers of the humble. In love, our Heavenly Father will answer our prayers by giving us that which will be best for us. It would be presumptuous to claim that prayer will always be answered in the very way and for the particular thing that we desire. God is both too wise to err and too good to withhold any beneficial thing from those who follow His will.

1. Read the following Scripture verses: Proverbs 15:8, 29; Matthew 5:44; Mark 11:24; Ephesians 6:18; 1 Thessalonians 5:17. What do these verses tell us about prayer? Do you believe that God is concerned about our prayers? Why or why not?

2. It has been said that God answers prayers four different ways: "Yes; No; Wait, or I've got something else in mind." How do you feel about this statement?

3. What prayers has God specifically answered in your life? What prayers are you still waiting for God to answer?

4. What are some of the keys to an effective prayer life? Discuss the places you go to pray, the way you stay focused and how to be consistent. What are ways you could grow in your personal prayer life?

5. Review and discuss the Lord's Prayer (Matthew 6:9-13) line by line. Why did Jesus share this prayer? Why do you think Jesus chose these different components in His prayer?

This week, memorize...

"Don't worry about anything, but in everything, through prayer and petition with thanksgiving, let your requests be made known to God. And the peace of God, which surpasses every thought, will guard your hearts and your minds in Christ Jesus." Philippians 4:6-7

Lord, I will faithfully go to my prayer closet and seek You. Help me to....

PROSPERITY

Recite the Scripture verse from the last study. What did God teach you this week about character?

Like most living legends, Julius Erving (Dr. J) is often asked about the greatest highlight of his basketball career. Though Dr. J enjoyed one of the greatest careers in NBA history with over 30,000 points scored, he likes to tell others what went on in his heart. He said, "At age 29 I realized I was looking good on the outside but was hitting a lot of peaks and valleys on the inside. After searching for the meaning of life for years, I found Jesus Christ. When I gave my life to Christ, I began to understand my true purpose. It's not to go through life and experience as many things as you possibly can and then turn to dust and be no more. The purpose of life is to be found through having Christ in your life, and understanding what His plan is, and following that plan."

Prosperity: Flourishing or being successful, especially pertaining to financial issues.

1. Who do you know that is regarded as a "living legend?" What did they do to get this title?

2. Would you classify this person as prosperous? Why or why not?

Team Builder (Optional): Invite a very successful Christian businessman or businesswoman to your team meeting. Work with your coach on identifying a good person from your community. Ask them to share with you the Top 10 reasons they achieved success (ask them to not exceed 15 minutes). At the end of their presentation, have a brief Q&A time with them.

Allyson Felix used to be known for her skinny chicken legs when her classmates watched her run in elementary school. However, all that changed when she began running track in ninth grade. She is still listed at only 5-foot-6 and 125 pounds, but she won't likely be mocked by anyone who has seen her run lately. She was only 18 when she stunned the world by earning a silver medal in the 200 meters in 2004. She was the world champion in three events in 2007 and is only the second woman ever to win three gold medals at the world championships.

Sports Illustrated writer Tim Layden wrote, "She wins with style, floating gracefully, rather than powerfully, as if the track is a bed of hot coals and she is trying to keep from burning her feet." Allyson's focus in every race is to bring glory to God. "I was raised in a very strong Christian home with parents that taught us to love the Lord and His Word. I came to know and understand that Christ died on the cross for my sins at a very young age. I have probably grown the most spiritually through my high school and college years. While there have been many changes in my life during the past few years, I'm still a work in process and the Lord isn't finished with conforming me to the image of His Son—Jesus Christ. The Bible teaches me that my priority should be to bring Him the glory regardless of winning or losing a race."

She stated, "When you recognize that your athletic career is in God's hands it can keep you from getting caught up in the 'winning is everything' philosophy that so many coaches and athletes follow in sports. Naturally, we all want to win or be successful, but unless we're doing our sport God's way, we're not honoring and giving Him the glory. Whether you win or lose, you need to realize that your priority or goal is to bring the glory to God. Once I understood God's perspective on sports it helped me to enjoy my sport and gave me a greater purpose for running."

Real prosperity is more of a condition of our hearts, rather than fancy clothes and expensive cars. God does promise to bless us with food, clothing and shelter as we seek Him (Matthew 6). Rather than manipulating and seeking after selfish ambitions, stay faithful and humble. Allow God to decide when you should be exalted and praised.

1. How has God prospered you and your family?

2. Have you done a good job of handling prosperity? Why or why not?

3. Comment on the following: "Real success comes not in thinking you've arrived at a place where others should serve you, but in recognizing that in whatever place you are, you have arrived at a position where you can serve others." What results when a prosperous person has an attitude of servanthood?

WRAPUP

For forty years the Israelites had wandered in the wilderness as punishment for their lack of faith. Joshua was now in command and ready to enter the Promised Land with a new generation of people ready to follow His lead. Before crossing the Jordan River to claim God's promise, God charged Joshua and the people to be devoted to God and His Word. If they would do this they would prosper. Throughout the first eleven chapters of Joshua we see that they remained true to God and His Word. Because of this they were blessed with overwhelming victories.

God desires for us to experience success. Scripture tells us repeatedly that He desires good and not evil, prosperity and not poverty, peace and not war for His people. Being promoted, noticed, praised and elevated to a place of prominence can come from God Himself. As Psalm 75:6-7 reminds us, "But God is the judge; He puts down one, and exalts another." Our true character often emerges through prosperity as we take credit for our successes. However, we should be quick to remember that it is not of our own efforts or good fortune but instead it really lies in the Lord's provision and mercy.

Though being prosperous is certainly appealing, it also can be a precarious position. Abraham Lincoln once commented,

"Nearly all men can stand adversity, but if you want to test a man's character, give him power." It's extremely dangerous to start believing your press clippings and believe YOU (apart from God) are somebody. Do you know what "EGO" stands for? Edging God Out! Unfortunately many people have stumbled terribly because they couldn't handle their success.

1. Read the following verses from Proverbs—13:21; 13:25; 22:7; 23:4-5; 28:20. What is the connection between righteousness and prosperity? What does the Bible tell us about the accumulation of wealth, trophies or anything besides God?

2. Jot down the names of four people who you think are successful. Put a word by each name that describes how that person handles his/her success.

After you've done that, discuss what you learned from this evaluation.

3. Rate your success quotient— what's more important? Why?
• Your level of success or your walk with God?
• Staying successful or keeping happy?
• Retaining a position or maintaining integrity or reputation?

4. What does God want you to do with what He has given you?

5. Not sure what you should be doing with your life? Here's some advice: "Take time for God, work hard and leave your future to Him." Look for verses in God's Word to support this advice.

This week, memorize...

"For I know the plans I have for you"—[this is] the LORD's declaration—"plans for [your] welfare, not for disaster, to give you a future and a hope." Jeremiah 29:11

Lord, I want to glorify God rather than seeking my earthly rewards. Help me to....

PURITY

Recite the Scripture verse from the last study. What did God teach you this week about character?

Troy Vermillion, a wide receiver, was cut from the Colorado Ice, an arena football team in 2007. According to the team, it was for performance; according to him, it was because he didn't like pornographic magazines and movies shown on the team bus. Vermillion is a devout Christian and he complained. He asked to leave the team bus and instead ride with his wife who was following the bus instead. The head coach told him he had to stay on the bus because he was a member of the team. Vermillion said that his playing time was cut that game and soon after he was released.

After being released, Vermillion stated, "It's all because I stood up. If I would have taken that movie to an office and made everyone sit and watch it, I would be fired. So

why is it okay for a football team to do it? I didn't want to bend my faith."

Purity: Freeing yourself from anything that contaminates or adulterates.

1. Was the stand made by Troy appropriate? Why or why not? If you were put in the same situation, what would you do?

Team Builder (Optional): Prior to the meeting, have several students interview at least one married person (perhaps a youth pastor) who waited until after the marriage ceremony to have sexual intercourse. Ask the married person for the keys to staying pure and the benefits they are reaping today from their commitment to purity. Share the positive and negative results with the entire group.

Ezra really impresses me. Here was a man who was responsible for re-building the city of Jerusalem after King Nebuchadnezzar and the Babylonian empire destroyed it. Israel simply "reaped what they sowed" as they were warned numerous times that there were consequences for their sins. Among the many sins they committed, they were impure. They intermarried with foreigners. Godly traditions were exchanged for filth. Their form of worship became bowing down to idols and false gods. Ezra stepped into this mess and dealt with these issues of impurity. He initiated a cleansing process, and the restoration of Jerusalem began to take place under his leadership. Read Ezra 9:1-15 and 10:1-17 for details.

One area that is particularly easy to become impure involves sexual temptation. God's Word deals directly with this issue and the perils involved when we do not rely on Christ's power and His promises. Romans 13:14 tells us "to not gratify the desires of the sinful nature." 1 Corinthians 6:18 reminds us to "flee from sexual immorality." We are pounded with impurity issues via the internet, television, movies, magazine racks, at the beach, park or mall. Certainly there are things we can do to protect us from impurity.

Jerry Kirk says, "Choosing to let Jesus be in control of your sex life will shape every other area of your life because sexuality is at the center of our being. This decision will influence your current and future ability as a husband (or wife), father (or mother) and Christian. Choosing purity is difficult, but for those who put in the hard work and prayer, living by Christ's standard is a road to deep joy and real sexual satisfaction."

Randy Alcorn says this about purity: "Purity is always smart; impurity is always stupid. Not sometimes. Not usually. Always. You're not an exception. I'm not an exception. There are no exceptions." Randy points out in his book, *The Purity Principle* that embracing purity is to claim a magnificent gift. He says, "To choose purity is to put yourself under God's blessing. To choose impurity is to put yourself under God's curse." Those are pretty big stakes!!

1. How would you define "purity?" Why does God highly regard purity?

2. Identify places or things that you believe are impure. Compare your list of items to what others have identified. Are you surprised what is and isn't on your list?

3. What are some of the keys to remaining pure?

WRAPUP

"If it feels good..." you can finish the sentence. The temptation of sexual pleasure outside of marriage represents the desire to be sensually satisfied no matter the cost. It may appear as harmless initially, but any sexual contact with anyone other than your spouse is an illicit sexual encounter. The inappropriate act is not the only issue; the attitude is the primary problem. "I want what I want when I want it. I am going to be happy. I need to be fulfilled; my sexual desires will be gratified...regardless!"

We may never come out and say it this boldly but we probably are thinking this way. In doing so we rationalize Scriptural truth, we lower our standard of morality, and we ignore the promptings of our conscience. We convince ourselves that it is not merely okay, it is a necessity! And if somehow conviction from a holy God interrupts the fun, we have ways of ignoring Him, too. Paul portrays such people as "fools" (Romans 1:21-22).

Daily we are told that sex outside of marriage is normal and a sign of true love. Our own longings for love and our God-given passions push us toward physical expressions of our feelings. But controlling passion is the best way to keep it strong and growing, even when you want to marry the person. According to the Bible, the boundaries of sex are the boundaries of marriage.

Sex and marriage go together. Honor God by staying pure...honor Him with your body (1 Corinthians 6:19-20). Finally, the battle for purity is won or lost in direct correlation between the time you spend with God versus the time you spend looking at or thinking about lustful issues. The more time you are seeking the Lord, the less time you'll put yourself in wrong places. Randy Alcorn said, "Do you want freedom from the actions and obsessions of lust? Get help. Be wise. Avoid temptation. Go to Christ. Experience his sufficiency. Draw on his power. Depend on Him one day at a time. Never underestimate Christ. Sin is not more powerful than God." This is good news for the person who wants to experience victory (1 John 5:4).

1. Read Proverbs 22:11; Philippians 4:8; Titus 1:15; James 1:14-15; 1 Corinthians 10:12-13; and 1 Thessalonians 4:3-7. Based on these verses, what are some of the principles God gives us regarding temptations and proper sexual conduct? What are the results of a pure heart?

2. How have you chosen purity over immoral behavior at school? In sports? On TV? At your job?

3. God created sex to be reserved solely for our mate within the context of marriage. How does sexual purity honor God? How does sexual purity bless us?

4. What is the key to remaining sexually pure? (NOTE FOR PARENTS: This would be an excellent place to discuss abstinence issues with your children).

This week, memorize...

"Even a young man is known by his actions—by whether his behavior is pure and upright." Proverbs 20:11

Lord, I am making a commitment to live a life of purity. Help me to....

RIGHTEOUSNES

Recite the Scripture verse from the last study. What did God teach you this week about character?

Steroid and human growth hormone (HGH) made headline news and even a Congressional hearing during the 2007 off-season. Seven-time Cy Young Award winner Roger Clemens used HGH, according to Major League Baseball's Mitchell Report, which cited information from Clemens' former personal trainer Brian McNamee. In an appearance before the congressional committee, Clemens denied under oath that he used HGH. His testimony contradicted former Yankee teammate, Andy Pettitte, who admitted he had used HGH before and that he was aware of Clemens' use of the illegal drug.

Righteousness: Acting in a moral and upright way that honors God, regardless of who is watching.

1. It seems like everyone has an opinion on the steroid and HGH controversy. What is your view on the subject? What do you think is God's opinion of this entire situation?

Team Builder (Optional): Performance enhancing drugs and alcohol have made their way into most locker rooms. Discuss the current state of affairs with your team on this subject. What can be done to eliminate the potential problems which accompany these inappropriate actions? What would be the right response by your team?

While Roger Clemens and his lawyers vehemently deny that Clemens ever used steroids, Andy Pettitte chose a different route. Pettitte came out and admitted he used HGH on two separate occasions. Andy Pettitte used HGH to recover from an elbow injury, the Yankees pitcher said after he was cited in the Mitchell report. "If what I did was an error in judgment on my part, I apologize," Pettitte said. "I accept responsibility for those two days." While it is commendable for Pettitte to make his admission, clearly it is too premature at the time of this writing to determine who is telling the truth in this entire scandal. As a man who has publically shared his Christian faith, hopefully Pettitte's righteousness will emerge.

How does Clemens feel about Pettitte's admission of taking HGH? Considering the two are close friends and are linked together in both the Mitchell Report and in Jason Grimsley's affidavit, would it be safe to assume that Clemens used HGH with Pettitte? Obviously, Pettitte won't face the same scrutiny that Clemens will receive and Barry Bonds has faced for years now that he's admitted it and apologized for it.

We have the opportunity to dramatically impact others through right behavior. Mark Twain once said, "Always do right. It will gratify some people and astonish the rest." Conscience is what leads a person to do right. A conscience is molded from the first lessons we learn about right and wrong. If we are never taught those lessons, we fail to develop a moral conscience. If we are taught poorly or incompletely, we develop a stunted conscience. If we override our conscience and refuse to obey its advice, we develop a hardened conscience, and over time, we will live as if we don't have one. Without a conscience, our lives are lawless, immoral, and tainted—without character.

We need to nurture our conscience by continuing to reinforce what we know to be right. One way to do that is to read aloud the Word of God and to hear it preached. I'm convinced that when our character and conduct are Christ-like, people will be converted. Another way to do the right thing is to simply meditate on the wonderful truths found in Ephesians 2:4-10. When I consider the benefits of right living it is a "no-brainer." For me, these are reasons enough to seek after righteousness.

1. How do you feel about Andy Pettitte's admission of use of HGH? What can we learn from his story as it pertains to righteousness?

2. Who do you think of when you hear the word "righteous?"

3. What does righteous conduct mean to you?

King Ahasuerus was seeking a queen to replace Vashti. Beautiful women were gathered from all over the province as possible candidates but his search ended when he found Esther. Early in Esther's reign, she was faced with a very difficult situation. Her people (the Jews) were to be destroyed by a decree from the evil Haman, who was the king's second in command. Esther was in danger for her own life if she revealed herself to the king. With an attitude of prayer and fasting, Esther stood up for righteousness and saved her people from destruction. Esther made a right decision because she had a right relationship with God.

Dr. Jack Graham said it like this, "Character is doing right no matter what the cost or consequences." William Penn stated, "Right is right, even if everyone is against it, and wrong is wrong, even if everyone is for it." From an eternal view, righteousness results in life and wickedness results in death.

Why is it important to do the right thing? 2 Corinthians 8:21 tells us, "For we are taking pains to do what is right, not only in the eyes of the Lord but also in the eyes of men." As this verse reminds us, doing right has benefits before the Lord and others. From the Lord's view, he delights in righteousness as noted in Psalm 15. Doing the right thing results in godly character and ultimately this will lead to obtaining the crown of righteousness which is one of the many awesome promises of Almighty God.

1. Read the following verses from Proverbs—10:2; 10:30-32; 11:21; 15:9; and 18:10. What do these verses tell us about the value of righteousness? List a few of the benefits of leading a righteous life.

2. Why is it important to be a righteous person? (Note: You might want to look up some of these verses to help with your answer: Deuteronomy 6:18; Psalm 106:3; Hosea 14:9; 2 Thessalonians 3:13).

3. Dwight L. Moody once said, "Character is what you do in the dark." Why is it important for your private life to match who you are in public?

4. Give an example of when you did "the right thing." How did you feel like afterwards?

5. Does your life honor God, or are you focusing on putting forth an image?

6. How can a person be "right" and yet remain humble? How can a person be "right" without becoming legalistic?

This week, memorize...

"Righteousness exalts a nation, but sin is a disgrace to any people." Proverbs 14:34

Lord, I want to be righteous before you as my audience. Help me to....

THANKFULNES

EXPRESSING GENUINE GRATITUDE

Recite the Scripture verse from the last study. What did God teach you this week about character?

Here are a few of the before you listen to this story (see "Team Builder"):

• Johnny MacArthur is Pastor John MacArthur's eldest grandson. He's a high-school senior at Hart High School and a scratch golfer with a full-ride golf scholarship to Pepperdine in 2008.

• Johnny is a senior, playing football for the first time in his high-school career. Of course, many well-meaning friends and conservative grown-ups advised him not to go out for football because of the risk of an injury that could jeopardize his scholarship. He tried out and made the team anyway.

• Hart and Canyon High Schools have one of the fiercest rivalries ever in US high-school football. Canyon was the defending California state champion in football.

Thankfulness: Expressing deep gratitude and appreciation to people and to God.

1. Share a time when you were thankful despite the circumstances around you.

Team Builder (Optional): Pull up the following internet link and listen to the story of Johnny McArthur (http://www.spurgeon.org/~phil /sounds/providence.mp3). Once finished, discuss your thoughts pertaining to Johnny's post game comments.

April is a special month for wheelchair racer Jean Driscoll. Since 1990, she has made an annual pilgrimage from her home in Champaign, IL to compete in the Boston Marathon. For her, it's the biggest race of the year. In the year 2000 she became the only person ever to win the Boston Marathon eight times. Success has not come easy for Jean. Born with spinal bifida, she has been an overcomer. Many years of training and a strong faith in Christ have helped her become the top women's wheelchair racer in the world. One of the many qualities that Driscoll possesses is a thankful heart. In spite of her physical limitations, she remains thankful for all of the Lord's work in her life.

Ten lepers approached Jesus pleading for His mercy and healing touch as noted in Luke 17:11-19. Jesus responded to their cry and healed them. Only one leper returned to Jesus to thank Him. Is this surprising? Not at all. Every day things happen to us that make us grateful and appreciative, yet we do not often express our thankfulness. Several years ago, I learned this was true. I sent a complimentary book to over 500 people, and less than 10% of these acknowledged the gift. Because of this experience, I have a greater understanding of the importance of being thankful. Since that time, I have made it a point to express my thankfulness whenever I am given the opportunity.

It would be easy to thank God for something that might save your life, but God expects His people to be thankful in all circumstances, for only He knows the beginning and the end. We need to express our genuine gratitude to God for His mercy, His abundance and His protection. We need to count our blessings and name them one by one. God has been so faithful and good to His children.

In the same way, we need to be thankful for acts of kindness and generosity that we receive from others. Aggressively respond with a thankful spirit when people bless and encourage you. You can never overuse the words, "Thank You." A lack of thankfulness can easily draw negative conclusions. You can actually wound people by withholding your thanks. Let others know how much you appreciate them. What a winning difference your words can make!

1. Name a person in your life who regularly expresses their thankfulness. Why are they so "thankful?"

2. Would you describe yourself as a thankful person? Why or why not?

3. What are you most thankful for at home? At school? In your sport? On the job?

WRAPUP

After nearly a year of controversy off the field due to unfounded rape allegations, the Duke lacrosse team returned to action in its 2007 season opener and defeated Dartmouth 17-11 before a crowd of 6,500. After reinstatement of the program, senior captain Matt Danowski was overflowing with thankfulness for the opportunity to compete again. "I can say personally I definitely appreciate it more. I took it for granted. We took going to the national championship game for granted. And playing games on Saturdays in front of fans, I took that for granted."

Is your life overflowing with thankfulness right now? Sometimes I wrestle with being thankful in situations I don't necessarily enjoy. When I don't have an attitude of thankfulness it's usually because I feel like I'm not getting what I want. However, when I take a step back and look at the big picture, I can see, by the grace of God, many things to thank Him for— primarily eternal life.

I encourage you to live and compete with an attitude of thankfulness today and every day, because no matter how good or bad life gets we know: (1) it is temporary, and (2) it doesn't compare to what we will experience in heaven if we have a relationship with Jesus Christ.

The Apostle Paul recorded some amazing words in Philemon 4-7 when he wrote his dear friend. Read his words of thankfulness along with the corresponding results. Being thankful served a great purpose, especially for Onesimus (See Philemon 10-21).

1. Read Psalm 69:30; Psalm 95:2; Psalm 100:4; Ephesians 5:20; 1 Thessalonians 5:18 and Colossians 3:15-17. What do these passages tell us about our attitude? What happens to others and us when we display a thankful heart?

2. What are some strategies you could implement to become more thankful?

3. Write out ten things for which you can thank God. Share your list with the team and discuss what you learned.

4. Write out ten things about your coaches, teammates or parents that you can thank God for. Share this list with this person(s). What did you learn from preparing this list?

5. Give each person a blank sheet of paper and have his put his name at the top of the page. Form a circle and pass each paper one person to the right. This person will write one sentence statement about their thankfulness for you on the very bottom of the page. When completed, fold the statement over so it can't be seen and pass the paper to the next person who will write something else. When the paper is complete, return it to the person whose name is at the top.

This week, memorize...

"But thanks be to God, who gives us the victory through our Lord Jesus Christ!" 1 Corinthians 15:57

Lord, an attitude of gratitude pleases God and it inspires others. Help me to....

UNDERSTANDING

GOD'S GOT IT ALL FIGURED OUT

Recite the Scripture verse from the last study. What did God teach you this week about character?

Without question, John Wooden is considered the greatest collegiate basketball coach of all-time. Wooden, known as "The Wizard of Westwood," won an unprecedented 10 NCAA titles at UCLA during a 12-year period (1963-75). The former All-American from Purdue is also a member of the Hall of Fame for his accomplishments as a player. One of Wooden's most remarkable traits was his ability to adapt in his understanding. He once remarked, "It's what you learn after you know it all that counts."

Understanding: Exhibiting strong intelligence and a sound mind in comprehending and discerning matters.

1. What role does understanding play in the development of character?

Team Builder (Optional): Visit www.coachjohnwooden.com and print off "The Pyramid of Success." As a team, discuss these principles. Look for areas where your team could put into practice the wisdom and understanding of Coach Wooden.

Wooden understood the importance of team unity. He stated, "I never permitted a player to criticize a teammate. If I saw a player criticizing a teammate I would, you know, uh, talk to him! I wouldn't permit that. I also insisted that a player never score without acknowledging somebody else. I tried to conduct myself in such a way that I wanted my players to act. I think our youngsters, whether they be basketball players or our children at home, need models more than they need critics. I wanted talking, but I never wanted any taunting. I see entirely too much of that today, and I think coaches can stop that if they wanted to. If I caught a player doing it, I certainly would not let it go unnoticed—he'd hear from me." These are a few of the "understanding nuggets" which Wooden proclaimed to his teams.

The lives of Philip and an Ethiopian eunuch intersected on a desert road in Acts 8:26-39. The eunuch was reading the book of Isaiah, but he was struggling with understanding it. Philip had an understanding of this passage, and he helped guide him to the truth. God used him in a mighty way to help the eunuch receive Jesus Christ as Savior and Lord. What joy both of these men experienced through understanding.

It is important that we do everything in our power to seek understanding. Like the Ethiopian, we need to seek out people and resources so we can learn properly. Like Philip, we need to be prepared to help others in their times of need. In their story, God provided answers that were understood. But there are times when the answers aren't easily found.

Chuck Swindoll says, "Frankly, sometimes God's heavenly plan doesn't always make earthly sense. Though we don't like to admit it verbally, we all think it, right? Sometimes His logic is illogical. Our understanding is earthbound and limited. Our focus is from the ground up. We are boxed in by the tight radius of time (as we measure it), multiplied by the circumference of logic (as we perceive it) and we operate in a dimension totally unlike our Lord....who knows no limitations. We see now while He sees forever. We judge on the basis of temporal, while He on the basis of eternal. We try to make all the pieces of the puzzle fit together, while God's logic is inscrutable, unsearchable and unfathomable."

1. Who do you know that seems to have good understanding? Why did you select him/her?

2. How is understanding demonstrated throughout the course of your day?

3. On a scale of 1-10 (1-Not Understanding and 10-Very Understanding), how would you describe yourself? Tell why you selected this number.

WRAPUP

Great teams and coaches are always looking to improve and grow. We are either growing in our understanding or we are stagnating—there is no middle ground. As a team, we must continue working and challenging ourselves to improve our performance. A "coachable" team is willing to critically look itself in the mirror and do the necessary things to learn from the past.

Some of my greatest character-building moments have occurred through my darkest experiences, simply because I learned and grew from them. I've been benched, demoted, rejected and mocked more times than I want to admit.

These humbling moments have proven to be some of the most teachable times. When handled appropriately, failures and disappointments can be a catalyst for understanding. In addition, a good thumping by a superior team can also be an excellent time for a team to take inventory on where improvement is needed. On many occasions, I have seen a total reversal in the outcome later in the year if a team is willing to correct past mistakes.

One of the most important Biblical principles you can grasp is found Galatians 6:7-9 on "sowing and reaping" (read it)!! Randy Alcorn summarizes it this way, "A holy God made the universe in such a way that actions true to His character, and the laws derived from His character, are always rewarded. Actions that violate His character, however, are always punished." If you remember this insight, your understanding will develop.

1. Read the following verses from Proverbs—2:1-6; 4:1; 16:22; 17:27; and 19:8. What does understanding do for us and our team? How does a person of understanding act?

2. What are things you or your team doing right now to help you gain understanding?

3. Which of the following do you do well in developing understanding and which one do you need to improve in? (1) Ask questions, (2) Listen, (3) Read, or

(4) Work Hard.

4. What is something specific from your life that is hard to understand or that you question God about? Have you trusted God with this issue and allowed Him to bring peace to your heart? Why or why not? (Note: After answering this question, read Proverbs 20:24. Sometimes the key to understanding is to accept by faith that God does have everything figured out, and we must trust Him with the results).

5. Name something in yourself, your life or your surroundings, that cannot be changed. Have you accepted this unchangeable thing even though you may not understand why God allowed it? If not, ask God to help you come to accept it, trust Him and use it for His glory.

This week, memorize...

"The LORD founded the earth by wisdom and established the heavens by understanding." Proverbs 3:19

Lord, I realize that good understanding saves me from much trouble. Help me to....

WISDOM

Recite the Scripture verse from the last study. What did God teach you this week about character?

Trent Dilfer has experienced both the highs and the lows that accompany an NFL career. He was the No. 1 draft pick for the Tampa Bay Buccaneers in 1994 and the starting quarterback for the world champion Baltimore Ravens in the 2001 Super Bowl. However, during his career, he's also occasionally sat on the bench. Trent retired prior to the 2008 season after a long and successful career. Yet Trent is wise beyond his years. He knows the most important source of wisdom comes from God. Check out his thoughts in the WARMUP to see a portion of his wisdom.

Wisdom: Learning to see and respond correctly to life situations and using keen judgment; the application of knowledge.

1. Trent has learned the key to wisdom—a personal relationship with Jesus Christ. Describe where you are at with Christ right now. If you are a believer, why is it important to keep your relationship with Christ real and active?

Team Builder (Optional): In advance of the team meeting, have everyone on the team do an interview with someone who's at least ten years older and have him or her share some bits of wisdom. Have everyone answer this question: What did you learn from this person?

Dilfer says, "Our society is one of self-promotion and self-empowerment, one where most people think they can do more good than bad, so they'll go to heaven. But that's not what the Bible says. We can't do anything in our own power to go to heaven. We need a way to pay for our sin. Jesus said, 'I am the way, the truth and the life. No one comes to the Father except through me.' We were created to have fellowship with God, but our sin gets in the way, so Jesus died a cruel death as the payment for our sin. He lived 33 years as the only perfect man, so He was the perfect sacrifice. Then, He proved He was God by rising from the dead three days later. He became our avenue to the Father, to heaven—if we accept Him as our Lord and Savior."

Charles Spurgeon defines wisdom as "the right use of knowledge. To know is not to be wise. Many men know a great deal, and are all the greater fools for it. But to know how to use knowledge is to have wisdom." Think of a time when you had knowledge (you knew the right thing to do), but you didn't make the wise choice. Why do we have this disconnect between our thought processes and our actions? In order to have true wisdom, we have to go to God's source—The Bible!!

What would you request if God appeared to you in a dream and said, "Ask for whatever you want me to give you"? That was the question He asked Solomon many years ago. Do you know what Solomon requested? (See 1 Kings 3:6-28 and 4:29-31). He humbly asked for a discerning heart to better govern the people and to distinguish between right and wrong. God was so pleased with Solomon's unselfishness, He made him the wisest king who ever lived—and besides that, He gave him riches and honor too!

Early in his reign, King Solomon's wisdom became known throughout the world when he dealt with two women who claimed to be the mother of the same infant. Because he was so wise, he was able to distinguish the truth as to who was the real mother, and people admired him greatly. His wisdom resulted in achievements, power, international influence and wealth.

1. Who do you know that is remarkably wise?

2. What are the ways we can successfully pursue wisdom? See James 1:5 for one possible answer.

3. Go back to the WARMUP and answer the question posed: "Why do we have this disconnect between our thought processes and our actions?"

WRAPUP

Over the course of Solomon's life, he strayed from wisdom and his life began to deteriorate as he continued to compromise and do wrong. He died as a man who said life was "vanity and chasing after the wind" (Ecclesiastes 2:26). His story reminds us that we must continually seek the Lord in our pursuit of wisdom.

Have you ever watched an icicle form? Did you notice how the dripping water froze, one drop at a time, until the icicle was a foot long or more? If the water was clean, the icicle remained clear and sparkled brightly in the sun; but if the water was slightly muddy, the icicle looked cloudy, its beauty spoiled. Wisdom is formed just like an icicle. Each thought or feeling adds to its influence. Each decision we make—both great and small— contributes its part. Everything we take into our minds and souls—impressions, experiences, images, or words—helps create wisdom.

Wisdom is something on which you must continually be working. You cannot relax. You have to continually pursue and cultivate this character quality every single day. The most important way to activate wisdom is to open up God's Word every day. Make it a habit to commit to a regular time for you and the Lord to spend time together. It will make an incredible difference in your outlook and help equip you in becoming wise.

Wisdom comes from God as a by-product of right decisions, godly reactions and the application of scriptural principles to daily circumstances. Wisdom comes from being faithful to the obscure tasks few people ever see. Wisdom comes from keeping your eyes focused on God and His Word. Psalm 90:12 says, "Teach us to number our days aright, that we may gain a heart of wisdom."

1. Read the following verses from Proverbs—2:6; 3:13; 4:5-6; 8:11-18; 24:3. From these verses, identify various character qualities that emerge when wisdom is pursued. What are some of the benefits of being wise?

2. What are ways we can successfully maintain wisdom? (Note: Consider the icicle illustration and the end of Solomon's life in your answer).

3. How can you apply wisdom at home? At school? In your sport and with your team? On your job?

4. What are some of the ways you've grown deeper in wisdom over the past year?

5. Tremendous insights can be gained through failure, adversity and disappointments. One of the great truths of our faith was made by Charles Spurgeon when he said, "As sure as God puts His children into the furnace of affliction, He will be with them in it." According to Charles, how does this saying relate to wisdom?

This week, memorize...

"The one who trusts in himself is a fool, but one who walks in wisdom will be safe." Proverbs 28:26

Lord, I understand that fads come and go; but wisdom and character go on forever. Help me to....

IMPACTING THE WORLD FOR CHRIST

Since 1954, the Fellowship of Christian Athletes has challenged athletes and coaches to impact the world for Jesus Christ. FCA is cultivating Christian principles in local communities nationwide by encouraging, equipping, and empowering others to serve as examples and to make a difference. Reaching over 2 million people annually on the professional, college, high school, junior high, and youth levels, FCA has grown into the largest interdenominational sports ministry in the world. Through FCA's "4 C's" of Ministry: Coaches, Campus, Camps, and Community and the shared passion for athletics and faith, lives are changed for current and future generations.

VISION

To see the world impacted for Jesus Christ through the influence of athletes and coaches.

MISSION

To present to athletes and coaches, and all whom they influence, the challenge and adventure of receiving Jesus Christ as Savior and Lord, serving Him in their relationships and in the fellowship of the church.

VALUES

Integrity   Serving   Teamwork   Excellence

Fellowship of Christian Athletes
8701 Leeds Road   Kansas City, MO 64129
www.fca.org   fca@fca.org   1-800-289-0909

FCA Ministry Fundamentals

FCA Ministry Fundamentals are Share Him, Seek Him, Lead Others and Love Others. The Ministry Fundamentals are the simple expression of what we are trying to accomplish. They are the foundations of all we do as a ministry. We believe that God has given us a ministry of evangelism to present (Share Him) the saving knowledge of Christ on the field, in the locker room and the hallways. We believe that once a person has come into a relationship with Christ there is the challenge (Seek Him) to be discipled in a life of walking and growing in that relationship. We believe that there are coaches and athletes that will accept the adventure (Lead Others) of developing their leadership skills in order to be a leader for Christ. We believe that healthy, loving relationships (Love Others) are also critical whether it is with family and friends or within the Church of Christ Simply put our Fundamentals can be defied as:

- **SHARE Him Boldly**

FCA shares Jesus with those who do not have a personal relationship with Him. We believe that salvation is only found in Jesus, and with great passion we desire to share the Gospel with the world. (Acts 5:42)

- **SEEK Him Passionately**

FCA equips and encourages others to seek Him daily. A life-long pursuit of knowing and loving Jesus takes perseverance and discipline. (Acts 17:11)

- **LEAD Others Faithfully**

FCA desires to model Jesus' example of serving by seeking out the needs of others, developing trusting relationships and caring about the individuals we serve.(1 Corinthians 14:12)

- **LOVE Others Unconditionally**

FCA realizes that the most powerful force in the world is love. We desire to be obedient to the Lord as He said that we would be known by our love. (1 Peter 4:8)

For more information or to contact FCA:

1-800-289-0909   www.FCA.org   fca@fca.org